This book
belongs to:

....

....

LET'S
TALK

The colours of the rainbow

Written by Jennifer Moore-Mallinos

Illustrated by Marta Fàbrega

SALARIYA
BH
BOOK HOUSE

There are lots of colours in a rainbow, each one different from the rest. All of the colours are unique and special, but side by side in a rainbow they make the most magnificent and beautiful sight.

Just like the colours of the rainbow, people are unique in their own special way. When people from around the world come together, they look just as lovely as a rainbow.

5

People may look different on the outside but they are all the same on the inside.

Some of us have dark skin and some have light skin.
Some of us tan nicely but some just get sunburnt.
Skin comes in many different shades and colours,
and each one is beautiful.

Our hair comes in all shapes and colours: every shade of brown, red, blond or black. Hair can be long or short, straight or curly, and we cut or comb it into many shapes. No matter how different our hair may be, we all have beautiful, colourful hair.

We see with our eyes. We all have two eyes but... all eyes are different.

Some people have round eyes and some have narrow eyes; some eyes are big and some are small. Some people have dark brown eyes and some have light brown. Many people have blue eyes, or even green.

We all like different clothes. Some people like wearing blue jeans, some wear saris, and some wear burkas, but we all wear clothes. Clothes help to keep us warm, but they are also a clue to who we are or where we are from.

13

The language we speak makes each one of us unique. Many people speak English, but there are so many other languages like Chinese, Spanish or Arabic. Some people speak more than one language.

We all use language to communicate. Even when we don't understand what others are saying, we all understand what a smile means. So, let's all smile!

We all eat, but we all like different foods. Some people like to eat pizza, but others prefer fried rice. Some of us like to eat pirogi, while others prefer curries. There are many different kinds of food, and trying something new is always exciting because it's different from what we usually eat.

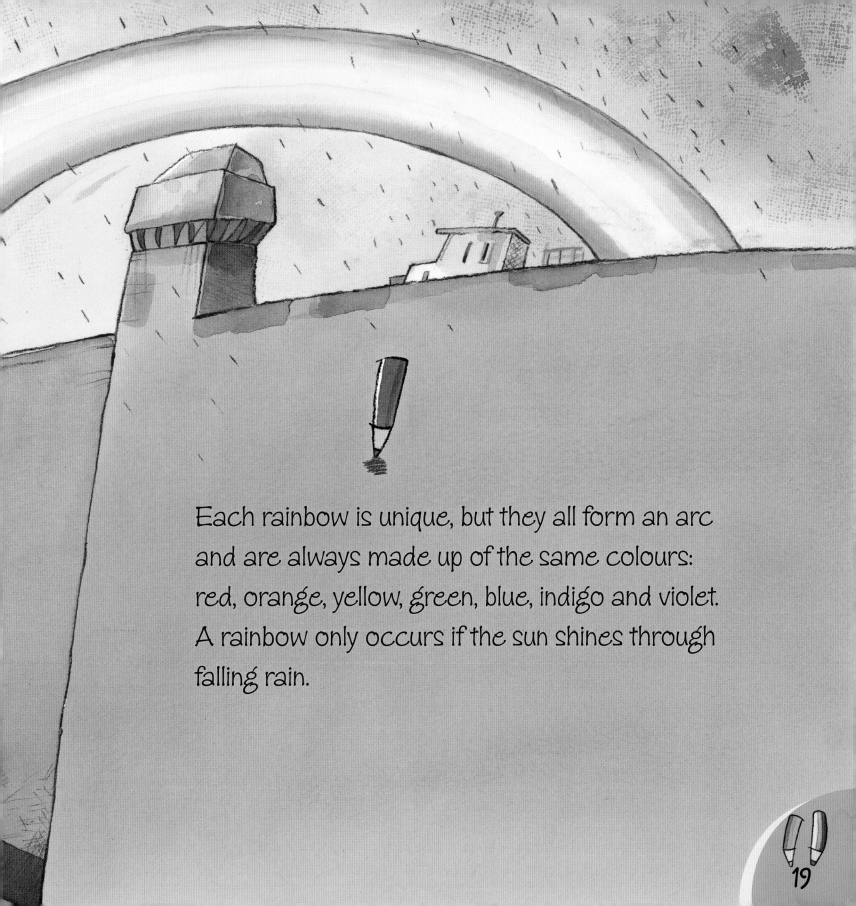

Each rainbow is unique, but they all form an arc and are always made up of the same colours: red, orange, yellow, green, blue, indigo and violet. A rainbow only occurs if the sun shines through falling rain.

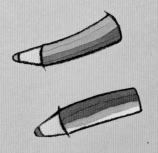

People are unique in their own special way, but, just like a rainbow, we all have much in common: we all feel happiness and sadness, love and pain. When we are happy, we smile, and when we are sad, we may cry. If we fall, we feel pain. A nightmare can make us feel scared, but when someone special hugs us, we feel love.

We each have a family who love and take care of us in the place we call home. Families and homes may look different on the outside, but inside they give us the love and warmth that makes us feel safe. There's no better place than home!

24

We all like spending time with our friends, playing games like skipping, marbles, hopscotch, or hide and seek. It really doesn't matter who we are or where we live: we all want to have fun and be with our friends while we grow up.

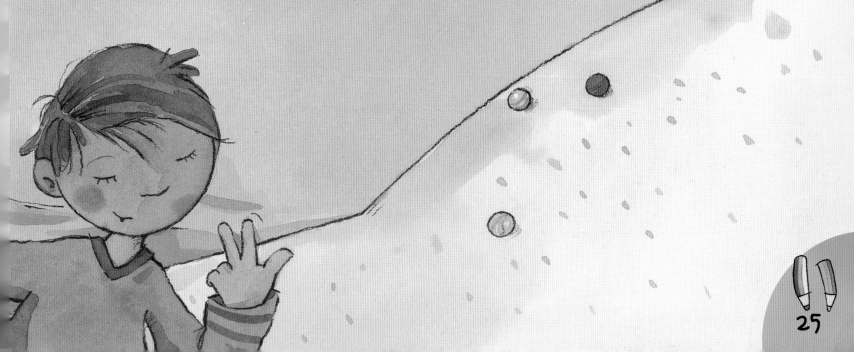

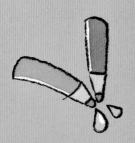

We all like to celebrate
special days that bring our
families and friends
together — special days like
birthdays or Christmas,
Ramadan or Hanukkah.
Whatever the occasion,
special days bring meaning
and togetherness into all of
our lives.

Just like a rainbow, we are all unique yet similar in our own special way. We all have skin, hair and eyes. We all wear clothes, eat food and use language to communicate. We all have feelings, thoughts, hopes and dreams. When we get hurt we cry, and when we are happy we laugh. When we are young we dream about the future, and when we are old we dream about the past.

Let's celebrate our differences!
Let's appreciate our uniqueness!
Let's come together and build a rainbow!

Note to Parents

We live in a world of great diversity where people from all places come together to build communities and to raise their families. As adults, we understand that people may look very different on the outside, but that we share more similarities than differences.

There are many colours in a rainbow, and each colour is different from the rest. Every colour is unique and special, but when they are side by side they form a truly wonderful sight.

The purpose of *The colours of the rainbow* is to acknowledge our differences, while at the same time recognising that there are many things about all of us that are the same. By accepting people for who they are and by appreciating their differences, we take the first step towards achieving harmony.

Use *The colours of the rainbow* to initiate dialogue and stimulate communication between you and your child. With your help, your child will have the opportunity to notice the many differences among people while also realising that people are more alike than they seem.

Let's celebrate our differences, appreciate our uniqueness, and come together to build a rainbow! Diversity is our strength, not our weakness.

Taking the time to read to your child is a wonderful way to share a moment together. Children are our future. What they think and how they feel matters. Our children will someday determine how cultures can come together in peace and harmony.

Let's show our children that we truly care!

Published in Great Britain in MMXIII by
Book House, an imprint of
The Salariya Book Company Ltd
25 Marlborough Place, Brighton BN1 1UB
www.salariya.com
www.book-house.co.uk

1 3 5 7 9 8 6 4 2

A CIP catalogue record for this book is available
from the British Library.

Printed and bound in China.

PB ISBN: 978-1-908973-22-1

Original title of the book in Spanish: Los colores del arco iris
© Copyright MMV by Gemser Publications, S.L.
El Castell, 38; Teià (08329) Barcelona, Spain (World Rights)

Other titles in this series:
My friend has Down's syndrome
I remember
Lost and found
Have you got a secret?
Daddy's getting married
When my parents forgot how to be friends
My brother is autistic